I HOPE SHE FINDS THIS

Also by r.h. Sin

I HOPE SHE FINDS THIS

r.h. Sin

Andrews McMeel
PUBLISHING®

VALE

You know the days when you can't see the sun, as it is buried behind clouds, or those moments during summer when it rains without warning? Those days when all your plans fall to pieces and frustration mounts itself to your heart? There's a sense of trouble waiting for you, but there's nowhere else to turn, so you run into obstacles and bumps in the road. You overthink yourself into a sinking pit of despair—hell on your brow, an ocean of tears ready to spill out the corners of your eyes. There's a silence that follows all of this, so quiet you can hear your own heart breaking, giving way to all the moments you've felt sadness but chose to run from it as you pretend to be okay. You know this type of day; you know this type of moment very well. Maybe you feel this way while reading these words, and maybe you're bracing yourself, trying to figure out how to prepare for the next storm. Though the toughest of days are unavoidable, you do know how to fight. You've been through a war like the one I'm expressing now, and I know you survived because you're holding this book; you're reading these words. No matter the weight of sadness, despite the overwhelming pain, you will always find a way out and on the other side of hell.

I couldn't sleep, kept up by my own voice and everything I didn't say. I doubt that I'd have another opportunity to tell you everything that sat silently within my heart when you were right in front of me. A part of me held back out of consideration for how you'd feel while the other was out of fear, afraid you'd have nothing to say while staring at the words from my heart spilled onto the concrete in front of my feet. I needed a second more to collect my thoughts before offering them all to you. And now I'm just lying here, lying to myself about what I would've done. I am filled with reasons why I must let this out but afraid to feel empty again since you're all that I have left, even though I no longer have you.

———————————————

It's so difficult to believe in the right type of love when all of your past relationships are evidence of how often you get it wrong when you decide to be with someone.

Do not hide what you're feeling; do not run from it either. You can't defeat your demons without facing each one of them.

it's strange the way
sweet melodies
can fill a bad song
or the way we search
for the right things
within a relationship
gone wrong

wanting to feel safe
but choosing insecure lovers
mistreated, beaten, bruised
thinking, "maybe they still love us"

You don't necessarily fall into love; you stumble a bit. Second-guessing every step because of what you've been through, and so I don't judge you for experiencing moments of fear as you attempt to get closer to the person standing in front of you. You're careful because you feel as though you've been careless. There was a time when you gave everything and lost it all to the wrong person, and so you tread carefully, afraid that you'll be running back into hellfire. I understand.

we're free
the freedom to choose
from whatever they provide
free to color where you wish
just as long as you stay
within the lines
speak freely; just don't say anything
that isn't written into your script
because if you're a freethinker
then everyone will get pissed

the poison
can't be the cure
the hand that hurt you
can't be the one you reach for
during trouble and pain

a fight for more.

you are going
to want to call them
don't

you'll feel that urge
to text them back
don't

no more reacting
to the bullshit
no more responding
to the manipulation

you're going
to want to give in
to everything you shouldn't
and that's like giving up
on yourself
don't

you won't find the sun
while settling for rain clouds
you will never feel the ocean
wading in lakes

you will never be free
believing those chains of lies
told to you not by a soul mate
but a cellmate
(misery wants you
to keep it company)

you need not allow
the keys of your future
to sit in the hands
of someone better off
in your past

the way toward true love
is through yourself
the way toward true love
is in the opposite direction
of the person
who is hurting you now
go

between the bars
sits a face with brown eyes
caged away in a tiny space
dreaming of freedom
waiting to get out
unaware that she's had
the keys the entire time

a piece of you
lives with me
like a ghostly reminder
of what happens
when you love
the wrong person

there is no war
too great
for women like you

the past is a home
for all the things
that should be left behind
it is not meant to be
a place for you to live

don't think about the past
more than you focus on the present

my room appears to be clean
but i stuck hell in the closet
and my demons beneath the bed
i smile, sitting peacefully
hoping that you will never notice
the pain in my heart and the troubles
in my head

heavy steps on thin ice
walking toward the eye
of a hurricane
just some examples
of how it has felt
trying to love you

eventually our hands
will grow tired
of keeping one another
from being
with someone better

your heart is heavy
because it's filled
with everything
you don't say

---

the heart can want something
that it needs to get rid of
and that is the trouble
with being in love

fuck off
if you intend
to half love me

i leave holes that sink
voids that can't be filled
i give the type of love
and devotion
that can't be replaced
a loss like me
could be felt for years
maybe an eternity

ask the ones
who chose to challenge
these ideas
they won't have to say a word
you'll see it in their eyes

remember this
the next time you attempt
to destroy us

the worst type of love
is one-sided
and it weighs heavily
on the shoulders of the person
who has always been deserving
of actual devotion
the weight of it all is so profound
that it nearly crushes the heart
that is open and willing to love fully
sadly, the person i'm describing here
has been you, someone who is brave enough
to dive into the unknown realms
of what love could be, only to discover
more of what love should never feel like
it feels right in the beginning, as it should
i don't think you'd open that door if you knew
the horrors that existed on the other side
so, what you find is a devil in disguise
a nightmare reconstructed to be a dream
and, in time, several truths
are revealed to be lies

you weren't concerned
about being a friend to me
when you decided to lie
what about when you chose
to fuck me over
as if i deserved those betrayals
so tell me why i should consider
keeping you as a friend
when you claimed to love me
but continued to hurt me instead

we all hear the word "love"
but many of us never feel it
we get told "i love you"
but rarely has it been shown

It'll happen without warning, and it'll hurt even when you saw it coming. Sometimes people walk out of your life before you're done loving them. Sometimes people leave before you're prepared to let them go.

_____

Don't confuse love with curiosity.

———————————————

No matter how complicated your past, you'll always have whatever you'll need to invent a beautiful future.

The love you deserve won't come easy. You'll have to love a few devils before heaven is found.

You knew they'd never love you, but because of the loneliness in your heart, you just wanted them to stay awhile longer, and that emotional truth, this feeling, is so fucking painful.

I wanted you to overflow my heart somehow, but you refused to give me enough of what I needed to feel loved, and I know it no longer matters; I know you don't really give a fuck, but I'm going to say this anyway. We could have been great, nearly magic, but you were too mediocre for my above-average ideas of love.

You don't get it. Did you not see the pain in my eyes? Have you not listened to my pleas for things to get better? I didn't want to leave; I needed to.

leaving you
was like trying
to remember myself

i let go
in an attempt
to find me

my nightmare
during day
a cold air
in june
i have hated
loving you

_____

It's just that when you finally see the bigger picture, you realize that some people will never have the frame of mind to fit.

We are not who we were when we first got here. You say I'm different, and I don't recognize you anymore. How did we become pieces of a puzzle that no longer fit?

heartache ages the soul
but after years of struggle
the mind now knows
who is worthy of being
thought about
and who is best forgotten

you have always
been stronger than
you knew you could be
and that alone is magic

---

too often
a lesson
in heartbreak
is taught to us
by the ones
we love
the hardest

travel far enough
that when your ex returns
you can't be found

"maybe" is a lie
we tell ourselves

————————————————

you love him
and it's okay
to change your mind
if he hurts you

The apologies came too fast. I should have known things wouldn't change because you never took the time to think about what you did or how it hurt me. And I forgave you too soon, afraid of being alone. Instead of holding you accountable, I was just eager to be held, even if by the hands of someone who no longer deserved to touch me.

what is meant
to be only yours
will find you

the heartbreak
has a way
of teaching you how
to fix yourself

what is gone
will never compare
to what will arrive
and that's a good thing

it ended because
you were too much
of a fool to love
and i was smart enough
to pack my shit and leave

the road is tough
but the destination
is worth it

what type of lie
have you told yourself
to keep you stuck
in a relationship
that has kept you
from being happy

you go from
just wanting something
anything to be honest
with time you discover
what it is that you deserve
and it's the most
disappointing thing to realize
that what you initially had
can never be what you need

in case you ever forget
there were mountains
that never stopped you
and storms you've overcome
there are demons
you've fought
until midnight
and won

It is never too late to start moving on.

you are a wild dream
and you deserve a love
that keeps you safe

You are not your broken feelings.

The stars are dead; don't wish on them.

It is better to have no love than to be half-loved.

a woman, in movement
is a dancing flame

───────────────────────────

When you walk away from the person who hurt your heart, you go from being alone to being alone, and the loneliness you feel after is so much better than the loneliness you felt while trying to love the wrong person.

When something bad happens, learn from it.

———————————————

When the mind is weary from overthinking, use your heart.

_____

The heart and mind can entirely trust a person, and it only takes one moment of betrayal to destroy that trust. Once altered, what is left is never the same.

You are most honest with yourself and others when you are tired. One day, you'll get tired of lying to yourself about a person who will never deserve your love and devotion.

Dear future love, please be better than what I've had.

People want roses but never have the time to nurture growth.

You expect the right things from the wrong person; that's why you're unhappy at this very moment.

we always pretend not to care
but we're always a long way
from not giving a fuck

it's scary to be the one
left behind, to be alone
when the one you wanted
more than anything
has decided to chase
someone else
and it is in that moment
when you discover
the peace in being without
the people who aren't
meant to stay

it didn't end like a poem
it was more like
a bad dream

you were never a soul mate
you were just in the way

---

i didn't come this far
to be treated so badly

i deserve something real
and that'll never be with you

---

everything looks like love
when you're lonely

Some people will never value your emotions; these are the people you should never waste your feelings on.

Deciding whether to try harder or walk away can trip you up a bit, but you must always choose the path that leads to peace when you're tired of the chaos.

_____

You fight for people who fight against you, making time for individuals who always seem to be too busy for you. This is why it hurts so bad; this is why sadness sits in the center of your soul. You often find yourself wanting those who don't even deserve you.

the demons
they come and go
without warning
they return unannounced
stronger than before
hungrier than ever
and my heart
is to be their meal

The other day, I realized that I'd had more scars than I'd been loved. And sometimes I wonder if I'm alone in this feeling. It's been difficult holding out hope for peace when most of what I've known is chaos.

toxic people are good at
making hell feel like a home
and this is what makes it harder
to leave them

never lose what you need
because you chose
what you thought you wanted

I'm listening to "Mad World" . . . and my heart is filled with goodbye. I've been struggling with the idea of losing you, afraid that if I walked away, I'd be forgotten. I have this fear that I'd be left on the shelf, collecting dust instead of your love and admiration. I'd fade toward the back doors of your mind until I was no longer housed in your thoughts. Made a memory that you rarely recalled, until one day, too late, you found these words and thought of me. I'm afraid to walk away, but I'm too tired to go on. You see, I've been at this for some time, too many years to count. And I've spilled these feelings, my heart, and these moments on many pages. I've written many miles to reach you.

sometimes
the hardest thing
to wear is sadness

I, for one, don't expect you always to have the strength to pretend to be happy. So, break down if you need to. Don't hide any longer.

The girl I wrote this for is a mystery to me, but from what I can tell from the rhythm of her pulse as she reads these words, she has a big heart, loves hard, and is capable of getting through the fog of feeling broken. She's been through it all, stronger than before, but despite that strength, she gets tired from time to time because caring for the wrong people gets exhausting. She's been in love and forced to fall out of it, pushed away even when she wanted to stay. She's been in pieces, shattered emotionally, and knows how it feels to be faced with the task of saving herself. She's misunderstood and often reads as a language that is hard to comprehend, the loneliness caused by loving those who won't even attempt to understand. But she is magic in a world that is hesitant to believe and even when she may not feel like it. She is more than enough, so much that she is everything she'll ever need.

fight of a warrior
strength of a queen

It's so sad when a child believes that they have to hurt themselves to get the attention of those they love more than anything. How lonely it must feel to be raised by parents who don't know how to be fully present because their parents weren't mindful when they were kids.

Maybe, as parents, we shouldn't focus so much on giving our children what we didn't have. Perhaps we should pay more attention to avoiding actions that take away the things that our parents took away from us. I can give my child the world, but what if kids are already born with it all, and, over time, they suffer a loss due to a parent's missed opportunity to make a difference? Show up when you're needed. Pay as much attention as you can so that you'll know when they need you the most.

––––––––––––––––––––––––

I tell my child that I am proud of him all the time; my adoration
doesn't have to be attached to some surface accomplishment. He's
only a toddler, and I find myself inspired by his will to connect, his
desire to communicate, and his ability to love without condition. I
am proud of the fact that I am allowed in his life, and I have been
given the opportunity to learn from him because even though he
stands at a height that reaches my waist and even while he doesn't
have a full grasp of our native language, he is my teacher. So, son,
if you should ever read this. I want you to know that I am so proud
of you. Thank you for allowing me the chance to love you.

in shared silence
i can hear my son's heartbeat
gracefully pacing through the moment
he looks at me with happy eyes
that whisper "i love you"
and this is how i define my joy
his presence like pillars
his eyes the reassurance
i didn't even know i needed

dancing without movement
whispers without sound
a language only spoken
by the eyes of someone
willing to be present
with a desire to connect

we look through silence
like windows into a warm room
welcoming one another
to be at peace
to feel joy
to be accepted
to feel loved

you know
despite the pain
it's okay to be lonely
being on your own
is the best way
to cultivate a love for yourself

I wanted it to mean something
but we don't always get what we want
and it is only once we see our losses
as something to gain that we realize
the difference between desire
and genuine needs

I think I drown the stories that would otherwise make me a burden to others. I drown these stories so deep that even I struggle to find whatever's left. And so, a part of me is always lost, incomplete, struggling toward the surface, weighed down by the guilt of fucking up someone else's life with my own. My silence an act of betrayal to myself and the emotional truths that live within my soul.

———————————————

I love the way you left me so that I could find someone better.

You were out looking for everything that I would have given you.
Maybe you should have just brought your ass home.

———————————————

I'm trying to get better at being more honest about what I feel, especially during bouts of depression. It's like I hate the idea of being a burden to others. So, I keep it all to myself, at war in silence.

_____

When a man says he doesn't deserve you, it's a warning. He's letting you know ahead of time that he will break your heart, and it will be devastating.

Friends with benefits only work if you're both reaching a climax. Otherwise, you're just assisting someone in their literal attempt at screwing you over.

Hopefully, you find someone who doesn't make you forget to love yourself.

I'm someone I don't want to be when with you, feeling things I hate because I love you.

I look forward to your attempts to replace me because it is then when you will realize what you truly lost, and when you return to let me know, I won't be here; I'll be gone.

Learn me like the moon knows a midnight sky. Take me in like lungs in search of air. Surround me like the ocean catching rain.

It's the middle of winter, but I see summer in your eyes. This is hell, I know it, but you bring a piece of heaven with you wherever you go.

I was lonely. It's not that I missed that particular person; I just missed having a person.

We'll be strangers again before I ever allow myself to be friends
with an ex who treated me like shit.

What a difference a year can make. Today, I'm looking back at everything that used to hurt my soul, knowing that the pain made me wiser, stronger.

When you go on to walk these streets alone, I hope you make it home safe.

New York, I still love you, but you feel different.

I tire of
watching you fall
deeper into the depths of hell
for a lover who could never love you

I've been here with you for so long. My words have seen you through the hardest of days, and you have carried me beside you for all the painful years. There is a peace embedded in these sentences, and every now and then, you find it. You use it to get through those moments of suffering and confusion. I was there when you first fell for the person who would turn out to be a heartbreaker, and I've been here for all the shit that came after. We bond over the heartache, maybe because I know what you're going through because I've suffered some of the same fate. I infuse those experiences, that pain into these lines.

I don't hate men, but I can see how a weak man who lacks proper comprehension may find it difficult to find messages that encourage women to be necessary and vital instead of threatening. Maybe my inspiration comes from growing up in a home witnessing my mother being abused, watching her struggle with being alone, then right back into the same type of relationship with someone different. That cycle hurt her, changed her, and may have affected me, but it was just hard witnessing it. Are all men horrible? No, I like to think that I try to be better and provide what is necessary and do what I can to be allowed to remain a part of my wife's life. But are there a lot of men who have manipulated good women or hurt good women? Yes, one of them includes my father, who also broke my heart. It's okay if you're bothered by my desire to hold my fellow man accountable for the bullshit while encouraging good women to move forward with their lives. But how can I hate men when I love me?

Canceled plans keep you stuck, correct? You keep trying and trying again for a person who isn't showing up with hopes that eventually something good will come from it, and maybe you both will do the things that were initially planned, but perhaps they're just a distraction from meeting someone you can actually depend on.

You'll hurt your head and your heart, missing the opportunity at true love by focusing on someone who isn't meant to be a part of your life. The right person will not come with mountains. The right person will come with whatever is necessary to help you over the obstacle. The right person isn't a part of the obstacle.

It's okay to find difficulty with fitting into certain relationships.
This is just a lesson of how to avoid going where you don't belong.

Tell the night sky you're not afraid of the darkness. Midnight is where you discover the candle that flickers in your soul.

You dance in the silence of uncertainty because you believe in your ability to endure and survive whatever obstacles are in your way.

―――――――――――――――――――

When you run out of excuses to stay, you are free to walk toward the door that will put you on a path to peace.

_____

nights are usually tough
so that the morning
can feel triumphant

You're reading this because you've possibly fallen for someone who decided not to fall beside you. Listen, some people do not dare to fall in love, and it's just that, in your bravery, you ended up in the arms of someone who uses their energy and words to hurt you. There's an endless supply of love and hope living within your heart, and so you stay longer than you should. You don't want to be alone, but you feel alone. You want to be happy, and it pains you to realize that the person you chose chooses to tear you down. Being with the wrong person keeps you from finding out what it would be like to be with someone willing to match your effort. You were strong enough to fall in love, and so you are strong enough to move on.

Being alone may be difficult at first, but I hope you learn to see it as a gift with time. The reward in being alone is to be without the drama of being with the wrong person. The reward in being by yourself is an opportunity to practice total self-love. When single, you are free and ready to discover your ability to be more than enough for yourself. You are also in place to have the opportunity to meet the right person.

It hurts, but it's the truth. Some of you will have to do it on your own for an extended amount of time, but it's essential to realize that you have everything you need to endure the struggles that live within the walls of loneliness.

You thought you left me alone, but, in all honesty, you set me free.

You thought you broke me, but, in reality, you showed me that I could stand without you.

I couldn't speak; it was almost as if I had wasted so many words that I could no longer communicate a proper sentence. My voice is nearly gone because of the yelling, my eyes tired of searching for sleep after days of madness, my mind wrecked from the thought of it all. Sometimes silence is the way; saying nothing is its own language in a circumstance like this, but something needs to be expressed, something that needs to be said, and it's fighting to be told. And so I write it here in hopes of being empty of you.

I think the heart goes to hell when it loves the wrong person.

———————————————————

Some days, you get burned; other days, you are the fire.

---

she's not a damsel
she's the knight

The trouble with life is that we spend a great deal of it entertaining people and things that have nothing to do with our purpose or that help us thrive. Too much of our time gets wasted in spaces that can and will destroy any opportunity at peace, joy, and progression. We give so much of the day to meaningless moments, then claim we don't have the time to do all the things that will enrich our lives.

some of what
starts like heaven
ends like hell

i still give a fuck about you
i'm just done fighting for you

I wasn't sad, but I wasn't happy either. There's a place there in the middle; that's where I've been for a very long time.

When you remain in toxic relationships and friendships that aren't worthy of your devotion, you exchange the truth for lies. You exchange everything you are deserving of to be in the company of people who don't deserve you. This is why the sadness within your heart won't cease; it continues to spread—growing in size, consuming every ounce of what joy you had left. And the only way to save yourself is to look beyond what you've felt. You literally have to look around the person who you love, as they've become a distraction, obstructing your view of whatever it is you've needed to see. You will have to leave the heartache of sharing time with those who hurt you just to enter another version of anguish, the one in which it hurts to be on your own, starting once more, but endings are pathways to new beginnings. And leaving will help you arrive at something real, a better relationship with yourself.

_____

You're too smart to be in love with an idiot.

don't fall for a face or a smile
smiling faces can be masks
fall in love with the soul instead
fall for the heart that is willing
to show you what love
can feel like when you've chosen
to be with the right person

forgive yourself
for treating hell
like heaven

You thought he was a piece of shit, but, with time, you realized he was a ton.

I wanted to tell you so many things, but I was silenced by the idea that what I was feeling would somehow burden you. There was a list of things my heart wanted, but you always seemed unwilling, but I stayed there beside you because I thought time would soften your heart. I actually believed that fighting for you, fighting for us, would be a war that I could win, but, in the end, what is a win without the reward, and what is love when you're with someone who hates you? So, I'll go into the night, carrying everything I came with. And I'll find a way to build a future without you.

I don't even remember sleeping, nor do I recall whatever dreams I've had. That itself is a nightmare, waking up from something you're unaware of. Tired throughout the day and restless beneath the moon. I'd fight harder for myself, but I just don't have the energy to do so anymore.

I get it; sometimes
you have to set shit on fire
so that you don't feel like ice

———————————

Isn't that one of the reasons why it's hard to move on? The heart that's been heavy throughout the relationship breaks and becomes not only difficult to piece back together but is also heavier to carry. You feel stuck because your emotions weigh you down.

Don't just stay with me; I need you to be better, to make an effort. I need some sort of change that would indicate that you belong in my life. I need to feel like I matter and that you are willing to hold yourself accountable for all the shit you put me through. I'm tired of wasting my second chances on the idea of us and the lies you've told. Stay with me if you are willing to be more than you've been. Let me go if you don't intend to give me the truth that I deserve.

_____

Sometimes, to find freedom, you have to detach from the person you thought you needed.

No one day is the same, and still nothing ever changes. I'm forced to forfeit the happiness I deserve because I believe that loving someone comes with sacrifice. There's a part of me that has held on for dear life, at war with the other half, fighting for the opportunity to choose my next move. What do I give in to, that impulse to fix you or the part of me that wants to leave you where you stand? I've been struggling for years now, or maybe an eternity, because these are the decisions I'm faced with making whenever I decide to get involved with someone. Either I'm good at picking people who are loveable despite the pain they cause or I seek out those who will have trouble loving me back no matter how much I give.

I've tired myself out, trying to figure out where I fit in this family.
And here I thought sharing blood with you would keep me safe and
out of reach of whatever lies you tell to manipulate those willing
to put their trust in you. I was somewhat blind, confused, and a bit
vulnerable. It was there all along, right in front of me, but I guess I
didn't want to see it. Who wants to believe that the ones they love
more than anything will also be the ones to destroy their spirit,
and the moment I let my guard down, that's exactly what you did.
But there's a lesson to be learned from all of this pain, yes, a silver
lining to everything that has happened. I realized that, in the end, I
didn't lose family; I gained another opportunity at peace of mind.

You mustn't allow the person you used to be with keep you from finding the person you're supposed to be with.

_____

It seems as though you weren't ready to give me the love I needed, and I was prepared to accept the fact that the future I wanted didn't have you in it. It was difficult, reimagining a life without you, but, day to day, it gets easier. The understanding that some people are anchors while others are engines. I didn't want to feel stuck; I didn't want us to remain stagnant. I wanted to grow, to move forward in love. I needed to evolve, and that meant leaving you.

A good woman is an intense fire illuminating beautifully beneath a full moon and a sky filled with stars.

you never meant
what i wanted you to mean
all this time, i believed in you
like some newfound religion
but you only intended to break my spirit
it's crazy the way we seek out peace
in the hearts of hell-raisers

if someone
makes you wonder
if you should leave, go

we'll never be
what we were
before the lies

i hope you get the chance to dance
in the rain with someone who remains
by your side no matter how tough the storm
someone willing to inspire peace
amid the havoc and pain

_____

I made peace with the fact that maybe I was never meant to be the destination. Perhaps I was always destined to be a bridge, connecting you to somewhere else, somewhere further from here. Our distance, the space between us, the larger it grew, the happier we'd both become.

I searched for the happiness you weren't able to help me maintain, and, on that journey, I kept running into myself. I knew true love all along; it was in my fingertips, beating within my chest. It was me this entire time, and I ignored myself to pay attention to you.

_____

The way you move on is by first seeing the relationship for what it has always been. The longer you avoid the truth, the longer it takes to break free from the prison of trying to maintain a relationship with someone who intends to hurt you.

the cure can't be created
until the poison is known

---

you want to feel wanted
it's lonely there, lying beside
someone who takes up space
in your life but refuses to be present
someone who barely uses words
to say they care and never enough action
to make you feel it in your heart

———————————————

the relationship is over
when the fantasy is running away

even though things
are different this morning
i still remember who we were
that night, under the moon
standing in the sand near the ocean
dreaming of a love that would never
become the nightmare that it is now

———————————————

i'll go because you did nothing right
wrongfully breaking me in half
a part of me wants to stay
the other knows it's best to leave
and so i'll go because you forced me
to be at war with myself
and if i stay, i'll lose half of me to you
and i just want to feel whole again

the answer is in the silence
the answer is in their absence
the answer is in their actions
people say many things
with no intent or desire
to follow through with what
has been repeatedly promised
stop looking for the answers
in the wrong places and soon
you will see the truth

you think it'll get better
it won't until you leave
you believe they'll change
but the heartache
remains the same each day
you think you deserve
this horror of a relationship
but you don't
and you will never know love
until you love yourself enough
to walk in the opposite direction
of the narcissist who has decided
to tear you down and distract you
from cultivating the happiness you want
you think many things
but in the end, you know for certain
what you must do to survive

and it's time to do it

you still hold out hope for real love
despite the failures of your relationships
because you are capable of loving
in the most profound of ways
and i hope you find someone willing
to match the devotion you give

you're brave
the way you continue
to be a good person
despite being mistreated
by bad people
and i hope life rewards you
with friendships you can lean on
and a lover who will genuinely love you

---

sometimes you have to be alone
relationships can wait

Red Flags in a New Relationship

Love bombing is an attempt to cover up mistreatment, disrespect, and or betrayal by showering a person with forced affection and attention. This can be used to confuse you and manipulate you into providing second chances to people who, in fact, intended to hurt you. Be careful.

Trust your instincts; trust your intuition. If you find yourself suffering from feelings of sadness, regret, emptiness, or confusion, chances are you're with the wrong person.

When you're the only one
taking the initiative, you feel
like you're doing all the
chasing. You make plenty of
the effort that rarely seems to be
reciprocated. This is when you
know you're with the wrong
person. This usually reveals
itself in the early stages of any
relationship. Usually, when
two people are genuinely
interested in one another, the
urge to make contact is on the
the same level of frequency.

Someone who makes you question your worth is someone you should avoid at all costs. This can usually be done to you by way of lying, acting cold and distant. Their constant mistreatment and disregard for your emotional well-being can often make you question yourself. These negative actions can also destroy the foundation of your self-esteem.

Narcissists have a hard time respecting boundaries. If you set boundaries and or express that you are uncomfortable with talking about or doing certain things and you find yourself feeling pressured into doing those things, you need to also understand that this person will have no regard for your needs and wants.

Stay away from individuals who
blame you for things that are
out of your control.

Stay away from people who manipulate you into getting their way by bringing up your past.

Stay away from people who get
upset over unreasonable things.
Avoid anyone who gets angry
with you for being upset over
something they've done to you.

You decided to read this for a
reason; trust that reason. I
know we don't know one
another, but I hope you find the
joy in being alone and being
with the right person. Finding
real love means letting go of
those who intend to hurt you.

3/22

last hour before sunrise.

i've been where you are
famished after dark
starved of all human connection
wavering beneath
this endless desire to be loved

cruel are the ones
who pretend to need you
until they find it convenient
to no longer want you

tossing you out like crumbs
unbothered by the fact
that they've reduced you to pieces

it is terrible when love hides its existence
and we, like fools, go searching for it
in relationships that resemble hell
and people who are just devils underneath

hidden parts.

i smile for my family
during daylight
then cry for myself
after midnight
alone for but a moment
long enough to hide
afraid to burden them
with the pain that throbs
in my mind and in my heart

they are not the reason
for this anguish
but they are a good reason
to keep it all hidden away

time, less.

what if time
isn't what we thought
what if these clocks
are more than an indication
of a current moment
what if the hands are waving goodbye
what if this clock
is just a countdown
that appears to be infinite
when it really isn't
but i don't think any of us
will be here when it decides
to run out of time

what it was.

sometimes i wonder
if you forgot the things
that i've remembered
like that first day of june
and that thing mid-september

decembers were always cold
with all the lies you told
a new year, the same shit
a puzzle piece that wouldn't fit

we go 'round like turnabouts
finding things to fight about
deeds done in the dark
then, one day, we find them out

we do this thing for several months
oh, fuck, maybe years
becoming nightmares to one another
and this was something that we feared

what begins as fun
is hell, until finally done
i remember everything
but am i the only one

You look up to witness the chaos that resides around you, and, now and then, you realize how chaotic it can be to cultivate inner peace when the things surrounding you are falling apart.

I was tired of the static; there was this annoying buzz whenever you spoke. The lies were too noisy, and the silence was what I craved.

I keep telling you that you should walk away, but maybe this time you should run.

In leaving you, I abandoned hell.

———————————————————

It all seems the same; the days don't feel any different until your future becomes the present and the past unrecognizable. Everything was changing, the love you had was fading, and yet you just found a way to fool yourself into believing that where you were was an okay place to be.

———————————————

a lonely heart
thirsty for anything
even a lie
as long as it
sounds pretty

it's just that
sometimes people
who aren't built to last
make promises of forever
to one another

I just want to make sense to someone willing to comprehend my heart's complexities for a lifetime.

the trouble with
a hunger for love
is that you lose
the logic needed
to decipher
what is real
and what isn't

some photographs
are of old lovers
who didn't last
faded on film
while others
are looked upon
with nostalgia
by the eyes
of lovers who
grew old together

right person, wrong time
that's how they try to keep you
maybe later, when the time is right
will have you stuck
waiting there for someone
who left you behind
to chase behind
your replacement

a toxic summer
is a lonely life
to live

it must hurt
to pretend
that empty encounters
are what make life fun

or that just fucking
for the hell of it
is some kind of heaven

and even if you won't admit it
the silence that follows you
is all the proof you need
to see that you're unhappy
despite doing what you thought
would bring you satisfaction
this feels like hell

you have a partner
and yet it still feels like
you're dancing by yourself

we went out into the world together
and i'm just trying to get used to
walking back home without you

the moral of this story
is that whoever breaks your heart
shouldn't be given the opportunity
to be loved by it after you've put
yourself back together again

go on, allow the fools
to criticize you for doing something
they'll never be capable of
let them speak on things
they could never comprehend
because in this life
many will talk
and only a few of us
will muster enough courage
to act, to do, to accomplish

ain't it crazy
how you can stop
believing in love
and still get your fucking heart
broken in two by someone
who could never love you

you are the shape of madness
you're cultivating rainstorms
and hurricanes
you have this look of tragedy
in your fucking eyes
and that smirk lets me know
that you've run through hell
and survived

you fall, you fight
you break on the way
toward victory
you've been quiet about it
you've yelled when the rage
inside your heart
could not be silenced any longer

and i love the fact
that you're holding this book
in your hands
refusing to give in
always ready for war
no matter how difficult
no matter how scary it can be
you are the badass
an inspiration to me

here's to the idea
of making up for all the time
we've lost in relationships
that were never meant to last

let's light a candle in the dark
and listen to one another
tell stories of survival
of what rivers of heartache
led us to one another

here's to the idea
that everything before this
was a lesson on how to be stronger
both as individuals and for one another

this is a toast to true lovers

your heart is heavy tonight
so heavy that your feet
could stand on the surface
of the moon, breaking all laws
of gravity

and i'm selfish because
i'm in pain yet overjoyed
that i found someone else
as hurt as me

may the cracks in our hearts
serve as lines on a map
so that we could briefly intersect
then maybe nights like this
wouldn't feel so damn lonely

it took me years of heartache
to realize that real love is homegrown
and in the event of being alone
true love can still exist

your name is a prayer
i say it to myself daily
like a mantra intended
for peace

some days are for breaking
some days are for healing
every day is a fight

you met me in the middle
where we were never
too much of any one thing
there was a balance
a safe haven
between the chaos and peacefulness
the wild and something safe

anything that ruins your peace
doesn't deserve a home
in your thoughts

it's no wonder
you find comfort
in demons
you're so used to hell

you've grown accustomed
to having your heart broken
and so it feels safer
to choose lovers
who will do what you expect
rather than feel the anxiety
and fear
of not knowing
what's next

it's hard to wear strength
when your heart is breaking
it's difficult to move on
when you're afraid of being alone

it was awful in the end
but it began
like a familiar song of hope

———————————————

we are so lonely
at times
that we hold on
to people
who make us
feel lonely
all the time

you were saying something
when you said nothing
and even though
you chose to stay
i knew you'd left
a long time ago

tell the girls
that they are still art
even when others
refuse to admire them

tell the girls
that there is a language
of love living within them
even when others
are incapable
of comprehending
what they've expressed

the scars
are struggles
carved into flesh
symbols of survival
messages of strength

sometimes "i'm sorry"
doesn't mean "i'll change"
sometimes "i love you"
doesn't lead to peace

It's difficult to see the "good" in goodbyes when you don't want to leave. This isn't easy, walking away from something you thought would last forever and leaving behind something you wish to take with you. But everything changes like the seasons in a year, so we've struggled with finding the courage to do the things we fear. Doors open when certain ones are closed; a new road opens up the moment you decide to switch lanes. I don't know exactly where you are on this journey, but I know that if you're brave enough to do something different, something better can happen to you. The beautiful thing about "goodbye" is that you gain the chance to say "hello" to new beginnings. And we can all benefit from a fresh start if we adopt this new perspective of letting go to begin again.

A sweet forever will never happen for the person who isn't willing to let go of those who sour their heart.

I hope you find a love that is greater than the greatest love you've imagined.

the silence
where i used to argue
the carelessness i felt
when it should have hurt me
that numbing feeling in my soul
when you said "i'm sorry"
damn, i was saying goodbye
all that time, but i never knew it

I hope you find someone who wants to be with you so badly that they're willing to struggle beside you with hopes of evolving and building something beautiful together. I hope you find yourself in a relationship that will outlast whatever doubt you've developed after being with the wrong person. When you decide to love again, I hope you begin with yourself, and I hope you challenge the next person who enters your life to match what love you've decided to pour into your own heart.

winter was harsh to you
but there are several summers
left in your heart

i hold her hand
i held the world

you never truly have her
when you're hurting her
she may stay with you
despite the pain
but she'll always belong
to herself
and as you break her
she'll be dreaming of a life
with someone better
someone else

my heart has been cold
for far too long
come see me soon
and bring your fire with you

look what the pain made you do
leave without regret
leave because you decided
to choose you

on nights when the moon
is not enough
you are your own light
a beautiful torch
in the darkest of hours

love is blind
and still
i hope you find a love
that you can see
hold and truly feel

a love that is wild
and safe
a love that inspires
your fire to keep burning

shit, it hurts
to see you smiling
with tears rising
in your eyes

but somehow you do this every time
when your whole world is falling and failing
you find a way to pick yourself up

and this is why i'm writing to you . . .

a love so transformative
that i became a canvas
as you touched me like paint

when you can't
find the light
become it

when you decide
to search
for something meaningful
don't forget to look
for yourself first

you are rare
too much
for ordinary men
with no imagination

you can't be cured
by the person
who chooses
to poison your heart

gone are the days
when i believed
in the religion that was you
wasted moments and time
emotions and energy
fixating on a future
that you didn't belong to
looking forward to something
i should have left behind

this is the last time, i promise
these are my final words
before "goodbye" leaves my lips
there are just a few more things
i need to express
before my heart's pen
runs out of ink

i stayed up all night to write this
18 minutes after midnight
and my dreams are calling

will you miss me
will you forget

i obsess over what will happen
in my absence; i've created
several scenarios

in which my departure
is just a daydream
a thought but not real

It's closing time; I can no longer serve my appetite to be near you. Crazily working for your attention, it's time we end this game we've been playing. I knew it would happen, just not so soon. Each day, extending hours out of hope and maybe a little fear, but, this time, I'm closing and locking the doors when I should. This time, I'm going home early, home, to myself. And to be honest, I have no intention of returning.

goodbye to empty promises
apologies that meant nothing
and second chances that were wasted

goodbye to being too afraid
to walk away to get closer
to something better

goodbye to giving hope to hell
relying on the hands that hurt you
to keep you from drowning

goodbye to everyone and everything
that held you back from discovering
the love that lives within
your own fucking heart

a love that when given to yourself
can and will set you free

goodbye to the pain
of choosing the wrong lovers
and expecting things
to somehow turn out right

you do know that saying goodbye
to all of these things
will mean saying goodbye to me
and these words

and so if it's "goodbye" to resonating
with the painful truths written here
then there's the "good" in goodbye

that moment when you no longer
need me or this book
that moment when you decide
to abandon hell for freedom

that fucking moment
when you find the courage
to give in to those urges
to leave the ones
who could never love you

that's when
we'll say goodbye
we'll drift away, old friend
and as much as I've enjoyed
communicating with you
we are not meant to last

i am just a stop
on your road to glory
i have always been
a resting place
for your weary soul

when you hold this book
you're holding on to me
and one day, you'll let go
and on that day
though a bit sad
we'll both rejoice

because you decided
that you deserve more
and i'm just happy
you gave me the chance
to witness you evolve

take care . . .

there is so much more
i wish to tell you
but i'm afraid
that i've run out of ink
and the pages here
can no longer
be written on

Andrews McMeel Publishing
a division of Andrews McMeel Universal
1130 Walnut Street, Kansas City, Missouri 64106

www.andrewsmcmeel.com

22 23 24 25 26 SDB 10 9 8 7 6 5 4 3 2 1

ISBN: 978-1-5248-7113-0

Library of Congress Control Number: 2022936532

Editor: Patty Rice
Art Director/Designer: Diane Marsh
Production Editor: Elizabeth A. Garcia
Production Managers: Cliff Koehler and Julie Skalla

ATTENTION: SCHOOLS AND BUSINESSES
Andrews McMeel books are available at quantity
discounts with bulk purchase for educational, business,
or sales promotional use. For information, please
e-mail the Andrews McMeel Publishing Special Sales
Department: specialsales@amuniversal.com.